...But I'm Distracted

Rachiel Renea

TRILOGY CHRISTIAN PUBLISHERS

TUSTIN, CA

Trilogy Christian Publishers
A Wholly Owned Subsidiary of Trinity Broadcasting Network
2442 Michelle Drive
Tustin, CA 92780

For information, address Trilogy Christian Publishing

Rights Department, 2442 Michelle Drive, Tustin, Ca 92780.

Trilogy Christian Publishing/ TBN and colophon are trademarks of Trinity Broadcasting Network.

For information about special discounts for bulk purchases, please contact Trilogy Christian Publishing.

Manufactured in the United States of America

Trilogy Disclaimer: The views and content expressed in this book are those of the author and may not necessarily reflect the views and doctrine of Trilogy Christian Publishing or the Trinity Broadcasting Network.

10 9 8 7 6 5 4 3 2 1

Library of Congress Cataloging-in-Publication Data is available.
ISBN 978-1-64773-644-6
ISBN 978-1-64773-645-3 (ebook)

Contents

Dedication

Jacob, Serenity, and Joshua–if I can, you can too! I love you!

RACHIEL RENEA

Introduction

How many times has God called you to complete a task but you seemed to get off course? How often do you feel a tugging at your heart to start that business, attend a church, move to a certain city, or leave that job? What is keeping you from following through? Is it a relationship? Fear? Cloudy vision? Or are you just not ready? What is it about the relationship that's holding you back? What questions do you have for God as it relates to the move? What's blocking the vision? I believe we all can agree when I say the real reason we can't do what God is asking us to do is that we are distracted.

Take a look at your current situation. Examine your growth from five years ago, two years ago, a month ago, last week. Are you constantly looking in the mirror, questioning your purpose? Questioning your 'why'? Then this book is for you! This is not one of those "read me and your life will be changed forever." Well, it just might...but this book also provides you with an opportunity to view life from a different perspective. It may actually confirm what you already believe but just have yet to implement.

When you are obedient to the will of God, you don't lose or miss out. You gain! There is a purpose in your location. You are not where you are by accident. God is very much aware of your talents, strengths, weaknesses, and qualities. That is why He has chosen you. "Mary Mary," a gospel duo, has a song titled, "Incredible." The songwriter expresses how much of a blessing it is to be uniquely chosen by God although feeling unqualified for the position. Exactly! It wasn't your degree or lack thereof. It wasn't the shoes you wear or the house you live in. God chose you because there's something in you that He wants to use.

I'm excited to journey with you as you learn more about yourself. I hope to encourage you and help you get back on track. I am always in the Bible bookstore looking for books to encourage me and motivate me. If this is your first time reading an inspirational book, I recommend you add more books like this to your library to be further inspired by different authors as you move forward. Of course, when you first pick up a book, you never know what to expect, but God has always given me what I need to push me a little farther.

I am single, and I have been all my adult life. I am often consulted by married and single friends and family about my thoughts and opinions regarding relationships. I enjoy having the opportunity to share all that the Holy Spirit has enlightened me on, and most have found it very helpful.

At the end of each chapter, you will have the ability to reflect on what you've read. Use this book as a tool to monitor your growth. Be sure to write down your responses to the questions at the end of each chapter, that way, a year or two from now, when you pick up this book, you can look at what you wrote today and see your spiritual progression.

Let me first caution you. If you are looking for someone to sugarcoat the truth, please return this book back to the bookshelf. I do not sugarcoat. When people seek me for help, it's because they are ready to accept the brutal truth.

Brace yourself! It's all in love. I wouldn't want you to spend another year wasting valuable time due to an unnecessary distraction. Let's ride!

Isolation

Yep! We have all been there. That time in life where we separate ourselves from everyone and everything. It's that moment when you feel like the world is against you, and no one loves you. You believe no one understands your pain. It's when you notice that everyone else's life just seems so perfect, and all you need is_____, or all you have to do is_____, and everything will be okay. During these moments, it's so easy to slip into depression.

When you're by yourself, quitting and giving up seem natural. It's the easiest time to walk away. On television and other media sources, we see that loneliness can end in suicide and has cost the lives of our favorite celebrities. We are in isolation by one of two reasons: choice or force. Sometimes, we choose to isolate ourselves. We don't want to be bothered, so we tend to avoid phone calls, emails, visitors, and so on. We decide when we are ready to deal with the world. Personally, I've gone to the extreme of changing my phone number and even moving. Yes, that's pretty extreme, but I'm sure someone can relate. Sometimes, isolating yourself can be positive if the reason is for personal growth, which brings me to my next point.

Isolation can be "by force." Do you recall times when you reached out to friends or family, and it seemed like everyone was too busy? Or how about a time when you felt like you were alone and no one cared about you? Was there something you did to cause the neglect? Probably not! How did you handle this? What did you say or do?

I'll tell you what you did! You acted out. You got mad. You texted mean things. You called and brought up old things from the past that have been bothering you and felt like this was the best time to speak on it. You complained about how nobody cares about you and that you feel like you don't matter. You probably even thought or said, *Maybe everyone would be better off if I were no longer on this earth.* You turned to drinking, smoking, or an old friend – you know the one I'm referring to. You didn't handle it well, and most don't! Allow me to enlighten you.

The Purpose of Forced Isolation

Welcome to the season of isolation. We, too often, rely on others or ourselves and very seldom rely on God. We have a tendency to pick up the phone and rant to our neighbor about an ongoing situation or have an evening out with our ladies, one in which we just feed off of each other's negative energy and complain about our situation, but to what effect? We can run to "old faithful" to pay a bill or to fulfill a lustful desire. We start with the *woe is me* sob story. Trust me, we have *all* been there! But that's not the purpose of this season.

It's during this season when the Lord has called you to listen. *What am I listening for?* I'm glad you asked! Direction! During this time, the Holy Spirit pulls us away from our friends and family so that we can grow. As we grow spiritually, we grow mentally. That means that some of the things we used to desire will begin to feel uncomfortable.

Like anyone else, I love a good time! I am loud and silly, but I must have my quiet time. This wasn't always the case. Before I understood the season of isolation, I felt like I was often being rejected. I would feel a tugging at my heart to read my Bible, but when I began to read, I felt like the Bible was telling me I had issues. You know, that same feeling you have when you are at church on Sunday, and you feel like the preacher is preaching directly to you and no one else? It was starting to get weird so I decided that I was no longer interested in reading what appeared to be "fun facts about Rachiel," and I would close the Bible with hopes of never returning. For weeks, the words from the Bible would play over and over in my head. I did my best to fight it. I kept denying the truth–*that's not me! That's not who I am!*

In my early twenties, I was a very arrogant and prideful girl. Not a woman; a girl. Life's experiences and growth in my spirituality have taught me how to be a woman. In my eyes, everyone was always wrong, and I had no faults. My heart was solid as a rock. I wasn't willing to listen to what anyone had to say, and I could care less if I hurt feelings along the way. You either loved me or hated me; There was no in-between. I was adamant about having my way and would go to any extreme to make sure I had it. I never took no for an answer. I was respected and feared; I loved it!

I was about 24 years old when I rededicated my life to Christ. I remember being led to read the book of Proverbs. I spent years reading and studying Proverbs. I didn't understand why. The Holy Spirit just kept saying, "There's more work to do in you." God used the book of Proverbs to reveal many of my evil ways. I kept thinking, *This can't be happening.*

The season of isolation can be challenging. We try so hard to fill the void by playing loud music, keeping a television on, or entering new relationships. We find anything else to do rather than spend quality time with God. Why do we do this? Because it's too quiet! We look at our phones like, *You've been dry all day!* It feels as if

God has closed off every line of communication—except His. How annoying, right? Wrong!

What a blessing! He chose you! You are "the called" that He is speaking of in Romans 8:28, "And we know that all things work for the good to those who are the called according to His purpose." God has a purpose for you, but how can you know what it is, if you don't spend time with Him?

Isolation is for your betterment. You not only learn who you are, but you learn who in your circle adds to your purpose and who takes from it. Anyone who takes from your purpose will begin to act differently as you make positive changes while those who add to your purpose will encourage you and push you to higher ground.

Think of isolation as a time of pruning. Jesus said in John 15 that He is the true vine, and his Father is the vinedresser. There are behaviors, people, and even objects that will need to be removed from your life so that you can elevate in Christ, fulfill your purpose, and receive the blessings that are in store for you.

Reflection Time

Think about the moments in life when you feel alone.
How do you fill the void? When you seek God, are you
seeking Him wholeheartedly? Write about your norm
and explain what you have decided to do differently.

_____

_____

_____

_____

_____

_____

_____

_____

_____

_____

_____

_____

_____

_____

_____

_____

_____

_____

_____

Where's Your Focus?

Distractions can come in all forms, shapes, and sizes. It's not always necessarily a person. It can be an addiction, social media, video games, or choosing to find things to do when you should be still. Let's talk about relationships! I am looking forward to my forever with my future husband; however, I have learned to be content with the fact that I am still waiting on him. In the meantime, I can't allow myself to get off track for temporary pleasures.

I have been asked by several men to marry them, but in actuality, I had no business with them in the first place! Those men didn't meet my standards, they weren't interested in a closer walk with Christ, and although I knew these things, I continued to entertain them, so they remained a distraction! Their purpose in my life didn't push me closer to God, and with them, I only ended up more hurt than when I started. Since

God wasn't moving at my speed, I thought it to be in my best interest to manipulate the process by trying to dictate which man was "close enough." I thought maybe if I encouraged the guy to attend church, he would be all I wanted, and life would be perfect! After many failed relationships and heartbreaks, I've decided to just leave that in God's hands.

Think about it! When these men who we think are "the one" come around, what are we usually doing? We are working on a closer walk with Christ, practicing celibacy, aligning ourselves spiritually, and are faithful in church. When we give in to the counterfeit, we stop doing all the above. Mr. Right is going to enhance us, not set us back. So, now we're distracted! One thing leads to another, and the practice of celibacy comes to a halt. I believe we can all agree that sexual intimacy can create a lot of distractions. Not only does it create distractions, but it also creates soul ties.

Soul Ties

Soul ties are created through any form of connection. I learned that it is important to break sexual soul ties before marriage. Have you ever told someone, "I'll always love you"? Yeah, me too! So, starting now, let's refrain from using those words with someone you are separating from.

When you confide in a guy about issues in your personal relationship, the sharing of these intimate conversations can create a soul tie, ultimately leading to an affair or the act of adultery. Promises are another form of soul ties. Have you had a man say to you, "I'll always be there for you no matter what"? I can't lie. That used to be my favorite phrase! If a man told me those words, I called him if I needed a jar of pickles opened! I'm just saying. But you are breaking soul ties, so instead, just tell him, "No, thank you! Take care."

I guess that's why the Scripture tells us to be slow to speak. Wow! God's Word seems to always circle back. Choosing to align yourself with God's will leads the enemy to be on standby ready to tempt you. This is called opening the door for enemy assignments. That simply means the enemy will send a distraction to keep you from fulfilling the will of God. The enemy knows our weaknesses too. That's why we must have a made-up mind to accomplish what God has assigned us to do.

Let's break these soul ties!

I like to listen to Jennifer LeClaire's ministries. It was through her teachings that I learned the importance of breaking soul ties. Jennifer shared that getting rid of gifts helps to break soul ties. Listen up; I've done this! As silly as it sounds, it works. I think it's more of the "out of sight out of mind" capacity. Have you heard of someone renouncing something in the atmosphere? All you have to say is, "I renounce [insert the vow/promise made/ relationship] in the name of Jesus." Renouncing allows the breaking of chains in the spiritual realm. Next, you want to repent for entering the soul tie. Lastly, forgive the person and yourself and receive God's forgiveness.

Soul ties are something serious! Clear your mind of these types of distractions. I encourage you to do any necessary research to enhance your knowledge on enemy assignments, renouncing unknown evil works in your life that you may not be aware of, and, of course, soul ties.

Fulfilling the Flesh

It's so easy to get wrapped up all over again in familiarity. Turning to what you know, even if you don't like it, is common because you already know the outcome and what to expect. How come we can't make the decision to step outside the box and trust that what God has for us will be purposeful? I believe it's because the unknown can be scary.

I've grown to realize that if I don't spend quality time with Christ, my entire day seems so off! I'll speak and act without thinking and create unwanted wedges in relationships. Later on, I'll be feeling embarrassed or trying to apologize for my outburst. I remember one day I called my sergeant to let her know that I was taking my infant son to a doctor's appointment. My baby had been throwing up and having frequent episodes of diarrhea. I had missed a lot of work behind this, and I needed to get to the bottom of it. During this moment, I was spiritually unguarded, and the conversation went in an unnecessary direction.

It was the season of Lent (a season of fasting for forty days). Lent is done annually, beginning at the end of February, leading you into Easter Sunday. Depending on whom you ask, the purpose and understanding of Lent can be different.

I had decided to fast from non-spiritual entertainment. Not even seven days into my fast, I found myself catching a flight to Charlotte, North Carolina, to attend a party for CIAA. Of course, I had an amazing time, but I was feeling convicted before I left home, before I attended the party, and on my return flight home. That morning when I called my sergeant, my flesh and spirit were warring, and it had yet to subside.

The sergeant didn't say anything rude, but because I was already dealing with me, her statement of, "We have to sit down and discuss your schedule because you just had a day off yesterday and now you are requesting a sick day," didn't sit well with me. I immediately took offense and got upset. At the moment, I felt like she wasn't demonstrating a sense of understanding. The truth is, because I was spiritually unguarded, there was nothing she could've said that would have made me react any better.

I drove to the office to express my frustration in person. I made it clear that I couldn't predict when my children get sick. I left the office feeling embarrassed and humiliated. When we don't arm ourselves spiritually, we become really weak.

Blaming Others

Though I've never been married, God has given me so much wisdom in this area. Often times, when we are involved with someone, we have a tendency to see any and everything that's wrong with that individual. You point out each other's flaws and shortcomings and hardly have anything nice to say. Sometimes, you probably have to sit and remember what made you attracted to that individual in the first place.

If you are questioning your relationship or trying to figure out how you got here, then let's first consider the foundation of the relationship. I am not convinced, and never will be convinced, that this man never showed you signs of (fill in the blank). Within the first ninety days and less than six months of a new relationship, you should be able to tell if a man is truly worth your time or not. I often hear married people say, "They were so nice at first and then after we got married, they changed."

Or maybe you chose to ignore or overlooked the signs of said behavior.

Did you include your lover in the important areas of your life or were there other deciding factors? For example:

- Meeting and spending time with your close friends and family, especially your children?
- Were you lost in the moments of passion?
- Does he have a lot of money?
- Is he extremely good looking, so you didn't care enough about your lover's attitude and behaviors?
- Were you tired of being alone?
- Were you just looking for a way out?

Bottom line—all those things are distractions! You were so caught up in yourself, what you needed, what they could provide, or your own circumstance that you just took the bait. Often times, many settle down just to say they have someone. Sex before marriage is a sin and obviously blinding. I know many people do it, but the fact that it can be so damaging is the reason God's design is so perfect! That's why it's important to involve God in everything that we do. Just because it glistens doesn't make it a diamond. Ask God the hard questions:

- Lord, is this man for me?
- Can you expose his heart?
- Can you show me what I can't see and allow me to believe it and accept it?
- If he isn't for me, can you provide a way out?
- Why am I choosing to be here? Expose my own heart.
- Does he meet my standards? Or am I choosing to lower them?

Nobody wants to accept the truth, but that's what sets us free. I'd rather know now that this man isn't worth my time than to invest all these years, have children, and create a home with someone unequally yoked.

Ungodly Counsel

A marriage is a love triangle involving you, your spouse, and God. Those are the only people that should be involved and making decisions in your marriage. I'm sure in many homes this is not the case. My sister always says opinions are like buttholes: everyone has one.

Psalm 1:1, "Blessed is the man that [doesn't] walk in the counsel of the ungodly."

There may be times when counsel is needed. You should never receive counsel from someone that says to you, "Girl, if I were you, I would—" Run! The only advice your counselor should be providing is Scripture. My niece, who recently married, has a lot of friends she enjoys hanging out with. The most important advice I gave her is to keep everyone out of her business. This includes family. You have to visit with family for vacations, holidays, reunions and you don't want anyone looking at your mate sideways. Eventually, this will create friction. Not everyone can deal with and understand that when you are venting about your issues that you are not looking for help. I have to ask my friends and family when they call me to vent, "Are you looking for an answer, or do you want to vent?" If they aren't looking for an answer, then I do my best to half-listen so that the details are foggy, and I don't really understand what's actually happening. Having loopholes causes confusion about what's really going on; therefore, I'm unable to pass true judgment the next time I'm with them and their spouse. Face it, I'm human too!

Obtaining advice from everyone creates a distraction, because not only are you unable to clearly hear your husband, you definitely will struggle to discern what God is saying. (Too many hands in the pot!)

The Bible is a mirror. It shows you what's wrong with you. When you are knee-deep in the Word of God, you are too busy learning about yourself and asking God to do a work in you. Your eyes won't be on your husband

and all his issues and faults. As a matter of fact, you will probably be too busy praying for the Lord to clean you up so that your husband doesn't notice your issues.

Paul reminded us that we are not fighting against flesh and blood, but against spiritual wickedness. These evil spirits have a tendency to step in and create confusion in our homes. The enemy's job is to cause you to go to war and fight amongst each other rather than going to God in prayer and asking that the holy angels fight the demons that are trying to take over your marriage and the structure of your home. You have to remember who the enemy is. Wives shouldn't tear down their husbands, and husbands shouldn't neglect loving their wives.

Fear and Doubt

Fear and doubt can cause us to take a different route. While God is leading us right, fear drives us left. In Joshua 1, God called Joshua to take the Israelites to the Promise Land. God's words to Joshua were to be strong, courageous, and fearless. Joshua was present to see the miracles God performed through Moses, so he had faith that God was being honest when He said He would be with him. As believers, we often see God's performance and miracles, but we still fall victim to fear. But we aren't the only ones.

In 1 Kings 19, we find Elijah running from Jezebel after God performed this amazing miracle through Elijah proving to the Baal worshipers that He was the true living God. Jezebel threatens Elijah's life, and out of fear, he fled.

David, throughout the book of Samuel, has his life threatened numerous times by King Saul. Out of fear, David is found hiding in the enemy's camp, in a cave, and in other people's houses. David was afraid for his life! King Saul was jealous of the calling over David's life to replace him as the new king.

Have you found yourself in similar situations? You want to know the best part about the prophecy of God over your life? It will come to pass! There's absolutely nothing the enemy can do that will remove the Lord's prophecy. The enemy will threaten you, curse you, attempt to defame your character, mistreat you, and possibly abuse you. But all of that cannot keep God's Word from being fulfilled. The truth is, nobody wants to endure the fight, because sometimes, it is extremely tough. Some people hear a prophetic word and, out of fear, immediately catch the next flight out of town to run away. Others tense up and become aggressive with anyone who reminds them or makes mention of the prophecy. I believe fear is one of the enemy's strongest tactics. It paralyzes believers. It will even cause you to question your abilities. God has not given us the spirit of fear.

Fear creates doubt. Doubt is the absence of faith. The woman with the issue of blood had faith that by touching only the hem of Jesus' clothes, she would be healed. There was no abracadabra or magic wand. Just believing made her sickness go away!

Thoughts help control our destiny. We *doubt* we will get promoted. We *doubt* we will get approved for the new car. We *doubt* our relationship will get better. We *doubt* God hears our prayer. Fear and doubt keep us from living our best life! The life that God intended for us. When do we stop thinking like this? I'll tell you when—now! Decide that there's nothing keeping you from accomplishing all that God has requested. Declare in your heart that even though you are afraid, God is leading you to a place of prosperity, and He will provide for all your needs.

If Abraham had never left his country, would he have been granted the opportunity to be the father of many nations? If Jacob had never returned home, would he and Esau ever make amends? If David never had a relationship with God in which he remained faithful and trusted God, would he have ever been crowned king?

Trials and tribulations in life prepare us for where we are going. God asked Jeremiah, "If you are unable to resist the people around you, how will you be able to compete with the horses?" Some of you are asking God to bless you to be famous, for promotions, for a baby, but are afraid to go where He is leading you. How do you know if the place He's calling you to isn't the door that provides the answer to your prayer?

Fear and doubt not only cloud our judgment but cause us to think in the natural. We are called to worship God in spirit and in truth. Don't allow science or the ability to put things into perspective distract you from God's supernatural abilities. The same God of Jacob, Isaac, and Job is the same God today. If he parted the Red Sea many moons ago, expect Him to part the Red Sea today!

While these are only a few of the many distractions that cause us to fall out from under the alignment of God's will, there are so many more! As women, our relationships, families, and careers are usually always at the forefront of our minds. We just have to trust God in these areas and believe that our prayers are reaching Him, and that God hasn't forgotten about us.

Reflection Time

Competition, trends, money, hair, nails, peace of mind. God cares about what you think, like, say, and do. How can you add God to your day to balance all the 'crazy' this world brings?

_____

_____

_____

_____

_____

Based on what you read, is there anything you will do differently in your relationships?

_____

_____

_____

_____

How have fear and doubt paralyzed your ability to fulfill your purpose?

_____

_____

_____

_____

Winds and Waves

Hang on for the bumpy ride! You're probably already riding! This ride deals with a rollercoaster of emotions. My younger sister always jokes and says that she's only seen me cry once or twice my entire life. Truth is—I'm a cry baby! Just ask my children. Have you realized that when you decide to choose God over everything, there tend to be interruptions in other areas of your life? It's like the minute you say, "Yes," friends walk away, children begin to act out, chaos rises on the job, and there's uproar in your marriage! The truth is that the enemy realizes that he is losing a member of his team and decides to do all he can to get you to question your faith.

Fitting In

I spent many of my teen years trying to fit in. People used to say, "You're not like everyone else." I have tried to fit in and act like people around me, but it felt weird. Nowadays, I find comfort in being around people who show and express love for Christ. This wasn't always the case. I used to enjoy drama and a lot of it. I was ready to kick down doors, make phone calls, snatch back stolen property—if it needed to be done, I was a phone call away.

I thought being overly flirtatious and wearing skimpy clothes was ideal. I believed the only way to attract the attention I desired was to dress and act like my friends. Did I turn heads? Of course! Anyone with eyes will stare at bare skin. If you're flaunting it, they will look at it! It wasn't until I became a woman (and remember, that has nothing to do with one's age) that I realized that confidence, beauty, and the Holy Spirit is what draws a *man's* attention to a woman. Now, this may not be your story, but in order for us to connect, I must be transparent.

When I made the choice to turn from my worldly ways, my flesh was fighting against what was right versus what I believed the world wanted. Why was this happening? Proverbs 16:3 reads, "Commit your works to the Lord, and your thought will be established." Through my connection with God, my spirit is able to suppress my flesh, which desires to appease the world. At times, this can feel like too much! Have you ever been trying to do the right thing, like biting your tongue when someone is persecuting you, and while you're trying really hard to maintain your faith and composure, you feel something on the inside of you rising? That's your flesh rising or warring against your spirit. Your spirit desires to do right, but your flesh says, *Act up!*

The Company You Keep

As you begin to grow spiritually and closer to God, everything that appeared okay will start to be bothersome. Certain conversations are no longer interesting. You notice certain behaviors in others that you may not have paid attention to before. Patterns that were once identified as the norm are now issues. You may start to question the evil ways about your partner that you once found attractive. This transformation in you will cause a separation between you and others.

Interactions amongst friends will change. Everyone can't remain in your circle. Your new behavior and mindset will push old friends away. If it doesn't push friends away, then you will need to purposefully separate yourself from friends that portray the "old you" to ensure you remain on the right track. *But we have been friends since kindergarten!* Yeah, that sucks! I'm sorry! Tell them, "Bye." That friend will do one of two things: (1) Join the bandwagon and want to develop a relationship with Christ too; or (2) Walk away.

My best friend and I have been friends since junior high. We were inseparable. We went to the same high school and college. She graduated from our HBCU, and I ended up pregnant in my sophomore year of college.

During this time, she and I both had deep, dark, personal issues in our lives that we were dealing with. She allowed her circumstances to push her closer to Christ, whereas I allowed mine to pull me away from Christ.

During this time, she learned to be abstinent while I became promiscuous. I was hurting, and I hated everything about life. She and I didn't remain in constant communication, of course, but each time we got together, her progression was a testimony. She needed to focus on her walk with Christ to maintain her stability for the path she chose. She never condemned me or said anything negative. She would share her progression, listen to my sob stories, and love me. She always told me she was proud of me, and that always encouraged me. As I made the choice to get closer to Christ, she and I began to hang out more regularly. I watched my best friend finish undergraduate and graduate school. I admired her passion and ability to remain faithful to God.

Ericka is another friend I met when I joined the Army at Fort Jackson, South Carolina. She was a hot mess, but I loved her spirit! I learned that she and I both attended the same high school. We instantly connected and made it our business to remain connected. After graduating from Advanced Individual Training (AIT), Ericka went away to Germany for a few years. When she came back stateside, Ericka found out she was pregnant with her first child. During that same time,

I had moved to Alaska, was engaged, and was pregnant with my second child. Ericka and I met up again in Charlotte, North Carolina, and from there, our friendship flourished.

We loved to debate. We debated about any and everything. My mom would watch us go at it and ask, "Why are y'all friends?" Easy! We challenge each other! Ericka eventually got closer to the Lord, and as she grew, I grew.

Maybe you and your ladies like the nightlife. Maybe you all like to create drama, date mad hitters, and post sexy selfies all over social media. We are all in different walks as believers. The best part is that God meets us right where we are and does a complete work in us. We just have to be willing to let him. I wouldn't find it strange if your lady friends told you that you're different or that you think you're better than they are. First, look at that word: Better. This is the term your friends are using to describe your change in behavior. Is this truly a negative statement? Not at all! It sounds a bit like jealousy. Not just jealousy, but a cry for help!

In my years of living, I have realized that the person who acts the hardest is usually the most sensitive. How do I know? You're speaking with the Queen. My encouragement to you is instead of arguing and fighting with the squad you once loved, lift them up in prayer. Pray that one day they will all turn from their wicked ways and know who Christ is for themselves. Proverbs 16:7 says, "When a man's ways please the Lord, he makes even his enemies be at peace with him." That's some good news!

You can't expect to move forward and get ahead if you stay in the same circle. You have to surround yourself with friends and accountability partners that are going to cheer you on as you flourish, pray for you, offer godly counsel, and help you move forward, if necessary.

Proof is in the Pudding

Are you ready for this? That tall, dark, and handsome fella you are spending time with may need to go! Let's discuss how ungodly men try to wiggle themselves into our lives. For my ladies who are single and dating, 1 John 4:1 lets us know that we are "not to believe every spirit." How many knuckleheads have you met that tell you, "I love God," or say to you, "You're celibate? I respect that! I find that sexy in a woman"? Then weeks later, he's telling you, *What you won't do, another woman will.* Friend, tell him, "Okay! Bye! She's out there! And good luck!"

Ladies! Quit falling for the okie-doke! That spirit is not of God. 2 Timothy 3 talks about these types of men. They like to meet women who are spiritually weak or don't know the Scriptures quite well and use it to their advantage. The Scripture identifies these men as lovers of themselves, unforgiving, slanderers, lacking self-control, lovers of money, and the list goes on! These men display a *form* of godliness, but they will take the Word of God and twist it for their personal advantage. Get this: Timothy even explains that these types of men will come into your home and take over—Run!

When you're alone or feeling lonely, the enemy will usually show up and say something like, "Girl, call him! You know you don't want to be alone." The enemy loves to play with our heads. Don't let him! Fight back! No, not with your hands. Fight using the Word of God! Tell the devil, "I stand on Hebrews 11:6; I have faith! I know my God will reward me for choosing Him. I stand on Galatians 6:9; I will not grow weary in well-doing. One day, I will reap the benefit of being obedient! I'm not alone, because Psalm 94:19 says that Jesus is my comforter!" Trust me, this will not be easy, especially if you often desire the attention of men and believe your validation comes from a man. Keep reading; I'll help you with some tactics later that will get you where you need to be. Stay strong!

The enemy loves to create turmoil amongst married couples. I will never condone divorce. I will advise wives to pray for their husbands. I encourage you to ask God to reveal things to you about your own heart. In 1 Corinthians 7, Paul speaks about how men and women who are married to non-believers can possibly win their spouse's soul for the Lord. The purpose of asking God to search your heart is to make sure that you aren't doing anything that will cause your husband to look at believers in a negative manner and that your actions are not the reason for the friction in your marriage. Think about your behavior. When the rough gets going, what actions do you display? I often hear married women say that they deny their husbands of sexual pleasures because they are mad at him, and he's in the doghouse. While that's cute, Paul also informs wives that they are to render the affection due to their husband.

If you are fasting, you definitely want to make your husband aware should God call you to stay from sexual intimacy. Believing that keeping your husband under control should be done by denying his flesh is not the way to go. Being cold-hearted towards your husband can create a stumbling block. Romans 8 reminds us that we cannot overcome evil with evil, but only with good. Demonstrating the love of God at all times confuses the enemy. The enemy is expecting you to be rude, condemning, and hateful. Displaying the love of Christ while the enemy is using your husband to fight against you is like heaping coals of hot ashes over his head. Your husband, who is still made of flesh and has feelings, will feel bad. Sometimes, when a person feels ignorant, it causes them to act out even more. But leave your husband in God's hands! Vengeance belongs to God.

Heartache, heartbreak, and pain are inevitable. There is nothing we can do to eliminate their arrival. The winds and waves of life are designed to create distractions and to strengthen you. You learn to wear blinders. You learn how to push through the pain. You remember to seek God in your heartache. Every day won't be perfect! God is always working! Even when it doesn't seem like it, He is. God's way is perfect! Don't allow the distractions in your relationship to pull you off your path. Ask yourself, *If I focus on this problem, will it hinder my destiny?*

Reflection Time

Take a moment and clear your mind. Release any negative thoughts. Ask God to reveal the people in your life that are pulling you from your purpose. Use the prayer template in the back of the book to record what the Holy Spirit shares. Pray for peace and liberty in your situation.

Read Hebrews 4:15-16. Remember, Christ was once in your shoes. He is our example of what 'right' looks like. Instead of running from your issues, take them to God.

Let us therefore come _____ to the throne of grace, that we may obtain _____ and find _____ to help _____.

Read Ephesians 5. Often times, we sin unknowingly. That's why it's so important to read the Bible. Remember, once you know what right looks like, God will hold you accountable.

Re-write the message in verse 17 in your own words.

_____

_____

How will you allow these words to reflect in your life?

_____

_____

My Prayer for You

Heavenly Father, this woman of God is beautiful on the inside and the outside. Lord, she belongs to You. She is faithful, grateful, and You know her heart. I ask that You hold her, keep her, and open her eyes that she may see You in each and every situation in her life. I pray that she chooses to accept Your revelations. I pray that You remind her that only You want what's good for her life. Lord, please give her the ability to be obedient, to walk in love, and to live a life of truth. Through Your Son, Jesus, I pray.

Amen.

When, God?

How often have you asked God this question? I can admit that, at times, I still do. No one likes to wait! The way our lives are set up, we can conveniently place online orders and expect delivery to our homes or offices within hours. This façade is not always the same as our Lord and Savior. Since God doesn't move as quickly as online order, we find ourselves upset, frustrated or feeling like He isn't as dependable as we thought. Therefore, people have a tendency to add Him to the "in case of emergencies" list. If the shoe fits, don't beat yourself up. This only creates shame and a further disconnection between you and God. Instead, quickly confess this to God and ask that He forgives you. Just like that, you are forgiven! Now, let it go and move forward! Our blessings can be staring us right in the face, but we can oftentimes miss it.

Are You in Position?

Take a look at the story of Mary and Martha in Luke 10:38. Jesus had come to the home of Mary and Martha for a visit. Martha was distracted as she was too busy trying to make a good impression for Jesus. In her mind, she believed that she needed to prove herself worthy by going overboard. The irony was that Christ, the houseguest, came to their home to be of service! Jesus had come to bring good news. Mary, on the other hand, sat at Jesus' feet to receive this good news. She was basking in His presence, taking advantage of His time and all He had to offer. Because Mary was still, she was able to receive. Distractions caused Martha to miss out.

Typically, we have one agenda, and then there's God's divine agenda. We oftentimes depend on our own understanding instead of seeking God for clarity and His understanding, resulting in wasted valuable time doing things our own way.

"Unless the Lord builds the house, they labor in vain who build it."

Psalm 127:1

"He who has ears to hear, let him hear!"

Matthew 11:15

It's important to be still. While you're still, you must listen. I have a friend who is probably the most 'still' person I know. While he's still, he's busy watching movies, surfing the web, or checking emails. To be still has two parts—seek God with expectancy and listen. You are to read the Scripture with expectancy and listen. Pray with expectancy and listen. Praise with expectancy and listen. The common denominator is to *listen!* God is always ready and able to give an answer, but the question is, do we position ourselves to receive the answer?

Idols

There may be distractions blocking your ability to receive your answer from God. In Psalm 139, David asked God to search his heart and expose sins that are hindering his ability to experience God's fullness.

My friend, Ericka, sent me a text one day and asked if I would join her for Bible study on Zoom. Zoom is an application that can be downloaded onto a Smartphone, which allows video conferences between two or more people. Without hesitation, I agreed to attend.

The focus of this particular Bible study was on idols. I was pretty sure I was aware of the few things in my life that I would consider to be an idol. I can see you're looking at that sentence like, *Is she serious?* Yes! An idol is any and everything that stands in the way of your connection with God. Your idol can be anything from

34

the amount of time spent in front of the mirror, ensuring your hair and makeup are on fleek to the numerous hours spent binge-watching your favorite series on Netflix. *Ouch!* I didn't mean to make you cringe. I was enlightened when Ericka stated that idols could also be our children. I paused a while and contemplated it. Needless to say, I was convicted shortly after.

I'm a mother to two handsome boys and a beautiful daughter. They are truly my pride and joy! Any opportunity I am afforded to spend time with my babies, I'm all for it—even if that sometimes means putting God's work on the back burner. I was putting my babies before everything. I'm sure you're thinking, *This isn't so bad. You sound like the ideal mother.* However, there are times I have been led by the Holy Spirit to go somewhere or do something, but because it didn't appeal to my children, in disobedience, I didn't go. I once told God how expensive childcare fees already were and that having to pay a sitter is doing too much! The truth is, I just wanted to spend quality time with my babies. Wow! So selfish!

I'm in no way proud of my actions, but in order for you to understand the ways in which we deny Christ or allow idols to control our thoughts, you know by now, I'm going to keep it real! You must first be real with yourself before you can get real with Christ. *Why?* It's His job to clean your heart. I had to accept that this was what I was doing, ask God to forgive me for putting yet another idol before Him, and request He helps me to walk in obedience.

Where's My Answer?

As much as we like to depend on family for guidance and support, they can also be idols. Have you ever called your mom or dad to assist you in making a life-altering decision? What was the end result? Did you end up following your gut or listening to their advice?

Ultimately, some people may go to God in prayer but run to the family for the answer rather than waiting for God to reveal His plan, which is sometimes for us to simply wait and to continue to pray. We take God either fully or partially out of the equation.

In Matthew 10:35-38, Jesus is speaking with His disciples, and He says,

> I come to "set a man against his father,
> a daughter against her mother, and a
> daughter-in-law against her mother-in-
> law; and a man's enemy is those in his own
> household." He who loves his father or
> mother more than me is not worthy of Me.
> And he who loves his son or daughter more
> than Me is not worthy of Me.

In these verses, Jesus is referring to idols, anything or anyone you put in place of God and His purpose. If we are honest with ourselves, we can admit that we have many idols we choose to worship. Have you ever considered your career as an idol? Are you overly committed to your job because you enjoy your lavish lifestyle, or maybe you are using your job as a way of suppressing your realities? We want the Lord to answer our prayers, but our faith and actions dictate His ability to move on our behalf.

Tithes and Offering

Let's talk about money. I recently had a conversation with my children about the purpose behind tithes and offering. My son had expressed that he believed I should stop paying my tithes because I was paying the pastor's bills. I told him, "If that's the case, then I'm ok with that!" Allow me to explain.

In Malachi 3:10, Jesus said we are to bring all our "tithes into the storehouse that there may be meat in my house." What does this mean? The church should be a one-stop-shop. You and I should be able to go to church and receive counseling, help with groceries or bill payment, attend available classes on personal, spiritual, and relational growth, and so much more. How does this happen? By you and I.

When I lived in Kansas City, I attended a church called Evangel. This was a pure example of a one-stop-shop. The church doors were always open! Pastors were available Monday-Sunday. I was updated weekly via email about the many activities the church was offering. The activities were funded for the attendees of the church and members of the community. I saw my tithes and offering at work through the adult, youth, and missionary ministries. I looked forward to paying my tithes and offerings because I never had to question where those funds were going. If you are involved in a church where you are unable to see your money at work, then I can understand your being hesitant about supporting such a ministry. Outreach should be the ministry of every church.

People very often misquote the Scripture in 1 Timothy 6:10, which reads, "For the *love* of money is the root of all kinds of evil, for which some have strayed away from the faith in their greediness, and pierced themselves through with many sorrows." Think of the stories we often hear about people who sell their souls to the devil just to be rich. I'm sure you have been a witness to people who bring down friends and loved ones just to get ahead for an extra penny or two. Politicians are oftentimes exposed in the media for wanting to cut a deal for money on the side. Careers and relationships have ended abruptly for an individual's love of money. Remember, God is your source!

You may be asking God for a financial breakthrough, and He's ready to provide it. Maybe He wants to increase your level of faith in Him by having you pay your tithes and offering. I used to ask God why I wasn't getting ahead. He led me to Malachi 3. I had read that passage in Scripture on numerous occasions, but I often read verses 8 and 9 and stopped. One day, I decided to read a tidbit further and found out that God petitions us to *try Him*. He explained that He would open up the windows of heaven and pour out a blessing so great that I wouldn't have room to receive it. I paused. I remember getting excited! I looked towards heaven and told the Lord, "God, I'm going to try You! Prove to me that I can trust You with my finances."

I started off with putting a few extra dollars in the offering on Sunday. I didn't see any difference. Then I increased my offering to ten percent of my net income or take-home pay. I remember looking in my wallet and saying, "Lord, I honestly can't afford to put this ten percent in church, because I won't have enough money the remainder of the week for the energy bill or gas in my car, but I'll do it anyway." I would leave church wondering if I made the right decision. As a result of my obedience, I found myself being blessed by others financially without even asking. I started receiving unexpected checks in the mail. I even watched my money that seemed like it wasn't enough, stretch! I was so excited! I looked forward to paying my tithes! I wanted to see what else God could do.

Years later, I was sitting in church, and the pastor was teaching on tithes. He explained that God expects us to pay ten percent of our gross income or the money earned before deductions and not the net income. I knew God was speaking to me through the pastor. I took a deep breath and said, "Okay, Lord. I trust You." I started to give ten percent of my gross pay. Again, I would look at my bank account and wonder if I would be ok. Today, I can promise you that I have not had to want for anything! I have such an overflow that I even asked God to allow me to be a blessing to those around me! People ask, where do I get the money to help others. I smile and say, "God has blessed me to be able to help." We must learn to be obedient and do what God has called us to do in order to receive our heart's desires. I encourage you to take a chance and increase your tithes. Watch how blessed you are from obedience.

Waiting Well

When we seek God for wants, needs, and direction, He often gives us instructions. Are you doing what God has requested of you, or are you providing Him excuses as to why you can't meet His request? You might believe that you are crossing every 't' and dotting every 'i.' If so, think about *how* you're waiting. Are you waiting well? Are you getting upset, jealous, or frustrated when others around you are prospering in the same ways you desire?

During my waiting seasons, I had a tendency of not waiting well. The inability to wait well happens, I believe, when we put a time frame on God's plan. It usually sounds like this:

"Lord, if my bill isn't paid by midnight, then I'll have to sell these drugs to make it happen. So, if You don't make a way, then it's Your fault if I get locked up."

"Lord, if Mr. Right doesn't come by the time I turn 30, then marriage isn't for me, and I'll just go back to being with Jason."

"Lord, this job isn't what I prayed for, and I'm so overwhelmed. I'm not going to stay here whether I have another job or not. Since You haven't allowed my resume to be selected for another position elsewhere, You must not care about my peace."

We often blame God for our delays, lack of opportunities, and when things don't turn out the way we expected. These behaviors do not represent waiting well. In Wendy Pope's book, "Wait and See," she explains that our waiting season should cause us to lose ourselves in Jesus. We should use this time to seek the Lord for growth and development. We should draw closer to

God through worship and praise, understanding that our outcome may be another season of waiting. I took her advice. I took my attention off my personal desires and asked God, "What can I do while I wait?" I enrolled in classes at a local community college to develop new skills for the ministry God is calling me to. I also used my waiting season to develop more spiritually.

We often plan ahead and fill out planners with appointments a year or two out. We have learned through planning and organizing that the day seems to flow a bit smoother. But what happens when things don't go according to schedule? It throws our entire day, week, or a month off! James 4:13 reminds us that we shouldn't arrogantly plan our lives, believing that things will go according to plan. Paul says our lives are a vapor. Don't waste precious moments bent out of shape because things aren't moving at your speed.

Philippians 4:6 tells us to

> be anxious for nothing, but in everything by prayer and supplication with thanksgiving, let your requests be made known to God; and the peace of God, which surpasses all understanding, will guard your hearts and minds through Christ Jesus.

"God resists the proud but gives grace to the humble."

James 4:6

Be excited when your friend or enemy progresses. Don't allow their behaviors or rewards to be a distraction. Keep your eyes on the prize! Do like Philippians 4:8 and think on things that are pure, true, lovely, of good report, and praiseworthy. When you have positive thoughts, peace follows. Your blessing is on the way! We all can agree that this is easier said than done.

When leaning on your own dependency, that's a true statement; however, if you trust God to change your focus by renewing your mind, then you can do all things through Christ who strengthens you.

Back in 2013, God had laid on my heart to create an errand service. I had come up with all the numbers and the necessary documents to move forward. I was told by a retired entrepreneur that my idea was too advanced, and that the world wasn't ready for it. Instead of adhering to his wisdom and guidance, I launched my business anyway. Not only did I launch it, but I also did it the way I wanted to do it with little or no guidance from the one who gave me the vision.

As we all know, today, there are numerous errand companies that are offering services similar to what the Holy Spirit has given me. If I had been patient and waited on the Lord, I would be financially set and on to the next business endeavor. Since the process wasn't meeting my timeline, I figured I'd help and do things my way. With my new business endeavor, I have learned to just wait on God. It's worth it—literally! Remove your time limit on God. Do what you know to do and what you can do.

"Wait on the Lord; be of good courage, and he shall strengthen your heart; wait, I say on the Lord!"

Psalm 27:4

Reflection Time

What is your personal request of God?

_____

_____

Wow! You wrote that down rather quickly! Now, His turn! What is His request of you?

_____

_____

_____

Did you have to pause and think about that? Were you able to write out the answer to His request as fast as your own, or are you unsure as to what He is asking you to do? If you had to pause and think about His direction or are unsure, then that's where you must start. Maybe you desire a godly husband. Maybe you've been praying for a wayward child. Your request could be that promotion on the job. Regardless of your desire, you may need to sit in the Lord's presence and listen to Him to find out what you first must do in order to receive that blessing your heart so desires!

Ponder on the following Scriptures.

"Trust in the Lord and do good."

Psalm 37:3

"Delight yourself also in the Lord, and He will give you the desires of your heart."

Psalm 37:4

"Commit your way to the Lord, trust also in Him, and He will bring it to pass."

Psalm 35:5

"Rest in the Lord, and wait patiently for Him; do not worry about the one who prospers in their way."

Psalm 37:7

How would you define your ability to wait? Is there anything you need to work on? Write about the steps you will take to accomplish your spiritual growth and personal development as you wait on God.

_____

_____

_____

Blessings in the Storm

As we discussed in the previous chapter, the moment you make the decision to choose God over everything, your normal gets interrupted and feels uncomfortable. As challenging as it may sound, you can truly find blessings in the storm. View your storm as its own distraction pulling your conscience and sight from the great opportunities, protection, and love that is being provided by God as you head toward your destiny.

Storms can be intimidating, and no one likes to be afraid. In 2 Timothy 1:7, we learn that God has not given us the spirit of fear, but of power, love, and a sound mind.

When your normal is altered, how do you typically address the change? Is it by cussing, fussing, quitting, fighting, arguing, and complaining? Does the complaining carry on for days, weeks, months, or years?

In the book of James, we are told to count it all joy when we are faced with any temptation or storm. Temptations are anything that may push your button and cause you to react according to the flesh. My motto is "blessings are found in storms." Guess what! You have to look for them. You have to purposely see God in your storm. If you seek, you will find!

In Matthew 14, we find Jesus' disciples in a boat wrestling with the sea. The wind had become very strong, and the waves were raging. I'm sure the disciples were really nervous and fearful of losing their lives. Jesus appears to the disciples, and He's walking on the sea. I can only imagine the relief the disciples had when they realized that Christ was in their midst. Close your eyes and remember a time when you were driving in torrential rains, and you couldn't see your way. Think about how soothing and comforting it was to see your street sign and know that you weren't far from home. In your storm, Jesus is in your midst.

So, in this story, Peter gets an opportunity to be a part of the action. Jesus allows Peter to not only safely get out of the boat as it's sailing, but He also enables him to walk on the sea. Now, remember, this is all happening while the sea is still raging! As Peter is walking on the sea, his eyes are focused on Christ, and he's excited! I can imagine him saying to himself, "I know the others are so jealous! I bet they wish they were out here!" As

Peter is walking along, his conscience kicks in and he realizes what's actually taking place. He looks to his left and his right, and he's seeing the rushing waters, and he hears the whistling wind, and he panics! Not only is Peter panicking, but he's also starting to sink. Peter cries out for help, and Jesus saves him. (Talk about an experience!)

Now, think about your life. One moment you're at the office, and life is good. Then, out of nowhere, you're being laid off. Where's your focus? Is it on the problem, or is it on God? Worrying causes you to lose sight of God, and you begin to sink into your own frustrations and anxieties.

In your storm, your faith has to be greater than your problem. God is the Alpha and Omega. This storm isn't a surprise to the Almighty. He was very much aware it was coming! Have you noticed that when one problem starts, two or three more begin to surface? You find out your spouse is seeing other women, or your child has been involved in an accident, or your car won't start. It's like when you least expect it, all hell breaks loose!

When I find myself in these moments, I'll go inside my vehicle and sit in silence. I just sit. I wait, and I listen. My car is like my sanctuary. I believe God and I connect so much better in that space. Is panic in my heart? Yes! But I run to my Daddy!

When I sit in the presence of God and just listen, I receive peace. How? Because my focus isn't on the current problem. Allow me to remind you: This world belongs to God. It's His job to provide for you and for me. Don't expect anything less than that. Expect! Expect God to heal your broken heart; expect God to pay your bills; expect God to feed you when you're hungry. If Jesus said He's the provider in Mathew 6, then let Him be just that. Expect God to protect your children. Expect God to do His work in your husband. Leave your issues at the altar and watch your strength blossom as you learn to depend on God in every way.

On this journey with Christ, we may lose a friend or two. Many days, we will be alone. Welcome to your new norm. You can't be like the world. You have the mind of Christ! It's hard at first because everyone else's life appears glamorous or joyful, and you're left all alone to deal with a hurting heart.

Let's take a look at a few Scriptures.

"Let this mind be in you which is also in Christ Jesus."

Philippians 2:5

"[B]ut we have the mind of Christ."

1 Corinthians 2:16

"Do not love the world or the things in the world. If anyone loves the world, the love of the Father is not in him."

1 John 2:15

"Casting all your care upon Him, for He cares for you."

1 Peter 5:7

"So do not worry, saying, 'What shall we eat?' or 'What shall we drink?' or 'What shall we wear?' But seek first his kingdom and his righteousness, and all these things will be given to you as well."

Matthew 6:31, 33 (NIV)

Unexpected Blessing

I had a Nissan Altima that I loved so much; I kept it nice and clean. The wheels were always shining, and I bought it at an amazing price, fully loaded! God blessed me with this car during a trying time in my life. One day, I had some work done on the car. It was almost time to renew the registration. I thought I was good to go until my check engine light came on. At that moment, I began to worry. I had recently lost my job and didn't have a consistent paycheck. I was making a little over three hundred dollars a month as an Army Reserve Soldier drilling monthly. Since I didn't have a job, I had grown more consistent in my walk with Christ. I was home reading my Bible all day, talking to God, or doing whatever I believed the Holy Spirit was leading me to do.

I took my car to the Nissan dealership to find out why my check engine light was on. I was told my car needed a new timing chain. It was going to cost $3000 to have this timing chain repaired. I drove away, very disappointed. My car would be paid off in five months, and now I needed to find a way to pay for a timing chain. I called my dad, who was a full-time mechanic, and got his opinion. I was hoping he would tell me there was a way around this, but he simply said, "No, ma'am." My vehicle registration eventually expired, and I started getting pulled over by the police 3-4 times a day. Some officers were friendly, and others were really harsh! I got rude with one officer, and he called for backup—I was so embarrassed.

Every summer, my mom would keep my babies in Texas so that I could complete my Annual Training with the Army Reserves. This particular summer, I had to figure out how to drive fifteen hours to pick up my babies with an expired license plate. I decided to have a conversation with God. I went into my sanctuary— my car—and began to ask God what was going on. *Lord, what is it I can't see? I don't have consistent income, but I trust You.* I decided to make one more stop and get the opinion of one more mechanic. As I drove to the shop, I felt like the Lord was telling me to go get a new car. I said, *Lord, if this mechanic tells me that my problem is my timing chain and that it will cost more than $1000 to repair, then I will drive to the dealership and get a new car.* As I'm sure you know, the issue was still the same. I pulled away slowly from the mechanic shop, and behind me was the police. I prayed that God would have mercy as I drove to the dealership, and He did.

I pulled up at the Mazda dealership because I really wanted a CX-9. I met with the salesman who took me on a test drive. This CX-9 was mine, and I wanted it! I told the salesman that I didn't want payments over $400. He explained that the monthly payments started at $450. We walked around the car lot, and he showed me a Kia Sportage. The SUV was three years old with 30,000 miles. The salesman and I took the Sportage on a test drive. I loved the interior and the smooth ride. The salesman said, "It's yours if you want it!" I took a deep breath and said, "Okay." My heart was racing because I knew the next few questions would be a show-stopper. I said nothing and walked inside the dealership. The salesman asked me what I did for a living, and I explained that I was a Soldier. As he walked away to speak with his sales manager, I began to talk to God. *Okay, Lord. You sent me here, so that means I'm leaving with this vehicle. This vehicle is Yours, so please give it to me.*

The salesman came back and asked me to provide him with a copy of my paycheck stub. My pay stub showed $342.00 for a one-month period. The salesman looked at me and asked, "Aren't you active duty?" I let him know that he was mistaken. He walked away and came back. He then looked at me and asked, "Can you afford these payments each month?" I told him I could. Brace yourself...I walked out that door with my brand-new SUV and didn't look back. Talk about a blessing in the storm! Thirty days later, I received a call for a full-time position with the Army Reserves.

God can see what we can't see! That's why it's so important to consult with the Man in charge. The enemy wanted me to think that my life was coming to a halt, but God wanted to bless me and prove to me that I can trust His plan. Sometimes, His plan doesn't make sense, but neither does sight being given to a blind man by Jesus spitting in mud and rubbing it on the blind man's eyes. I could've called a friend and asked for their opinion about what I should do. I could have taken matters into my own hands and gone to the bank for a loan to repair my car and missed out on not only my blessing, but a miracle. The best part? I can share my experience with you!

Distractions cause us to become literal thinkers. We feel like everything needs to be taken into perspective. We check bank accounts, look at gas tanks, rely on temporary feelings, and we line up all those facts against our situation. When we do this, we limit God's ability to be great, because we are relying on the things of the world. You are probably thinking, *That kind of stuff doesn't happen to me.* I must ask you a few questions: Are you impulsive? Do you react without consulting God, or do you consult God and react without an answer from Him? Are you being obedient? Trust me, everyone is going to have an opinion about your life and what you do. It's only what you do for Christ that matters!

Behind the Scenes

When the storms of life arise, don't you feel like running away? Maybe you have. I know you can't necessarily run away from your spouse or send them away, but what can you do to hide in Jesus as your storm is raging? Jeanette, a family friend, married a man who was not equally yoked. He wasn't in the church and wasn't interested in learning about who God is and what He could do for him. Jeanette continued to show love towards her husband. He would tell her he didn't want her attending church because she was always in service. He tried to come in between her relationship with God. Jeanette felt torn. She didn't know what to do. Often times, she questioned God about her marriage. Regardless, she continued to show love and continued to attend church. She didn't allow her relationship with her husband and his jealousy of her love for Christ to get in the way of her walk with God.

Jeanette flourished spiritually! This once shy woman of God was leading ministries in her church, receiving financial blessings, and ministering to coworkers at her job. One day, Jeannette's husband became very sick. His sickness had become so bad that he was hospitalized and no longer able to work. Jeanette would go to work during the day and spend the evening with her husband in the hospital. Jeannette used this opportunity to bring her husband to salvation. God sustained her marriage, and her husband gave his life to Christ. Consistency with Christ in any storm is the key! Your focus on God's abilities rather than your own inabilities will grant God the opportunity to perform miracles before your eyes.

Storms will rise. We can't do anything to stop them from happening. Living in a bubble won't save you. Storms are made to develop you. In Christ, you find the strength you never knew existed! There is healing in storms. There's protection in storms. Your breakthrough is in a storm. The only way to get over your past is to get through your storm. Reliving the pain and memories of the past can be so daunting, but you won't go through it alone this time. You can seek refuge and comfort in God. Someone out there has experienced your hurt. Pray that God leads you to sound, godly counsel that will further you along. He will!

Reflection Time

Make a note of your many fears, then turn to the back of the book and give these fears to God in prayer.

_____

_____

What will be your new approach to your storms of life? Write about the expectations you will have of God moving forward.

_____

_____

_____

Is there anything in your past or present that you need healing from? Is there someone at church or in your life that can pray with you or walk with you through your healing? Journal and express to God your pain. Listen to the Holy Spirit as you write to see what guidance He has to offer you.

_____

_____

_____

_____

_____

_____

Help Me Focus!

We can remember to plan for family reunions, annual cruise vacations with the ladies, Sunday gatherings during football season, and quarterly retreats. Now, let's create a routine that will help you rejuvenate your mind, body, and spirit while strengthening you to move forward.

It's important to start each day with Christ. Surrender your ways to His ways each day. Let God know you want His will to be done on earth as it is in heaven. Ask God what your day will be like. Request God to prepare you for what lies ahead in your day. Ask the Lord for protection.

Prayer

Praying means to talk to God. Think of prayer as a place where you can run and hide. Praying is the spiritual connection between you and Christ. It is what creates the relationship between you and the Savior. When you talk to a friend, you feel connected when you can learn new things about that person or when your friend feels comfortable enough to confide certain information in you. It's the same with Christ. When you share your thoughts, feelings, ideas, and moments in life with Him, He opens up to you just as much! Opening up to God about what's going on with you and asking Him to move on your behalf indicates faith. When you pray, doors open and doors close. Habakkuk 2 tells us that the "just will live by faith." Hebrews 11 describes faith as the ability to hope and believe in things that we can't see at the moment. After His resurrection, Jesus told Thomas that you are blessed when you haven't seen yet believe.

There are different levels of praying. As you grow in Christ, your prayer life will be elevated. Some people have been in church all their lives and are still praying the same prayers they prayed as a child. Remember, the purpose of your walk in Christ is to grow.

When you pray, you fight in the Spirit. Our adversary is the devil. He comes to steal, kill, and destroy. Since the devil is a spirit, we can't use guns and knives to attack him. Therefore, one of our supernatural weapons is prayer. I was listening to the radio one day, and Pastor Tony Evans's ministry was playing. He was discussing the importance of prayer. Pastor Evans expressed the wickedness and warring that takes place in the spiritual realm. In the book of Daniel, chapter 10,

Daniel seeks God for the understanding of a vision that he received through the Holy Spirit. Daniel prayed and fasted for three weeks as he waited for his answer from God. In the third week, an angel came and awakened Daniel and explained that God sent the angel with the answer to Daniel's prayer in that same hour, but the enemy, which the Scriptures identify as the prince of Persia, was fighting him and holding him back from delivering the message that God had for him. The angel said the fight was so bad that he had to call for backup. So, one of the chief princes, Michael, came to help him fight.

Let's think for a moment. If Daniel had decided not to pray or fast to get his answer, how much longer would it have taken for the message from the angel to be delivered? It was Daniel's fasting and praying that gave the angel strength and the backup he needed to get the message delivered in a timely manner. Wow! If this is not an eye-opener...

Ponder on this Scripture.

The righteous cry out, and the Lord hears,
and delivers them out of all their troubles.
The Lord is near to those who have a broken
heart, and saves such as have a contrite spirit. Many are the afflictions of the righteous,
but the Lord delivers him out of them all.
Psalm 34:17-19

Prayer is a key to unlock doors. 1 Thessalonians 5:17 tells us to "pray without ceasing." Talking to God throughout your day allows you to remain connected. Without intention, you will notice your day lines up. When it looks like things are falling apart, praying will add comfort and assurance that everything is going to be ok.

As believers, we are constantly attacked by the devil with hopes to keep us from accomplishing the will of God through distractions. We have supernatural body armor that we must wear to protect us as we go through each day. In Ephesians 6, Paul informs the believers that we have to remain battle-ready! Our supernatural body armor is known as the "whole armor of God."

Helmet of Salvation

Since we have the mind of Christ, our thoughts should reflect salvation. We must think about things that are true, noble, of good report, anything worthy of praise. The tactic of the enemy is to change your way of thinking. The enemy desires you to feel defeated before you start. The enemy wants you to be afraid and deem your purpose as impossible. The helmet of salvation must be worn to protect your thoughts.

Breastplate of Righteousness

As natural human beings, we do not have what it takes to look like Christ. We must depend on the strength of

God. When we put on the breastplate of righteousness, we are afforded the supernatural strength to show love even to our enemies. Remember, the enemy knows your weaknesses, and once you let him in your head, he then wants to get under your skin, causing you to act in your flesh, which makes you and others question who you say you are in Christ. Wearing the breastplate of righteousness helps you to be able to display Christ in every situation. In 1 Thessalonians 5:15, we are told not to do evil for evil, but to pursue what is good for yourselves and others.

Gospel of Peace

On your feet, you must wear the gospel of peace. There will be times when you would want to run! There will be times when you would want to quit, and times you might quit. Psalm 23 tells us that God leads us beside the still waters. Anxiety will set in when things start to get chaotic. It's the nature of our flesh but find your peace in God and stand on it! Don't allow the faults, guilt, shame, or momentary defeats get you off course and shake you from your peace in God. 1 Thessalonians 5:16 tells us to "rejoice always!" Praise and worship will be your peace. When you can't shake those negative thoughts that the enemy plants in your head and when you feel the flesh rising, and you want to do evil for evil, find your peace! The Holy Spirit will put a song in your spirit, sing it out loud! The Holy Spirit will give you the Scripture, say it out loud! Stand on God. He will keep you in perfect peace!

The enemy will send messengers to tell you all types of lies. It may sound like, "You are a loser!" "I knew you couldn't do it!" "You are all alone!" "You are unlovable!" "You won't make it!" When you know who you are in Christ and what you are entitled to, no devil in hell can stop you! When you believe that you are more than a conqueror through Christ, you can keep pushing. We will get weak and make mistakes, but our sins are forgiven. You are redeemed by the blood of the Lamb! You are predestined for greatness. Before the foundation of the world, you were already chosen! You are holy and blameless through Christ. You are crowned in glory. You are beautifully and wonderfully made. In order to have faith, you must have something you believe in. Believe in Jesus! Jesus is all you need!

Belt of Truth

A belt is used to connect or hold something in place. The belt of truth keeps us intact. Should you choose not to start your day with Christ or to not set your mind on positive things, and when something unexpected comes your way, you will almost always lose your mind. Think of the high suicide rates. I'm sure if those individuals that committed the act of suicide had a chance to share why they decided to take that particular route, they would probably say they thought their whole world was falling apart, and there was no way out.

You're still here, and since you're still here, sit for a moment and ask yourself, "Is my world falling apart? Will I be able to bounce back from this?" Then think about the other moments in your life when you may have had the same thoughts and feelings. Friend, if God did it before, I have "mustard seed faith" that He will do it again! The enemy attacks when we are both weak and strong. The only way to keep it together is by holding on to the truth.

Sword

Inside the belt of truth, is the sword. Here's where those prayers come in! Your sword is the Word of God. How can you know the Word if you're not reading your Bible? Any time someone recites a Scripture, whether you are at church, with family, or friends, always look up the Scripture. People will twist the Word of God and even use it out of context. We must study to show ourselves approved. We must have the Word of God in us in order to properly display it. Otherwise, you can only display the ways of the flesh. 1 Thessalonians 5:21 tells us to "test everything and hold on to what is good." God's Word is what keeps us together. It's what maintains our faith. God's Word is what helps us put on and display righteousness. God's Word is what allows us to stand strong and be at peace. God's Word is what changes our way of thinking.

Shield of Faith

"So, then faith comes by hearing, and hearing by the word of God."

Romans 10:17

Faith is the absence of fear. When you pray, you have to believe what you pray for. Otherwise, your prayer is in vain. Believe that God's Word is true and that God will do what He says He will do. Use the shield of faith as your protection from the many lies which the enemy will throw your way while trying to convince you that God won't and can't move on your behalf. Instead, remind yourself of all the ways that God has already made. When you think about the goodness of Jesus, you can shout, "Hallelujah!" and hold your shield high when the enemy tries to deceive you. Cover yourself with the shield of faith when the enemy wants to retract anything good and the prophecies over your life. Trust that God is not slacking when it concerns His promise!

I know it sounds like a lot, but when you put this into practice daily, it becomes second nature. As you dress yourself each morning, practice putting on your spiritual armor at the same time. And just like riding a bike, you will never forget. The enemy's job is to create distractions. The enemy is doing his job even when you aren't doing yours. On days when you wake up late, still pause and make time for God. Thank Him for allowing you to get up late. Don't grab your phone, and don't think of any excuses to tell the boss. Just talk to God. He has you covered.

True story: I was home praying to God one morning about my day and was seeking God for direction. As God was giving me directions, I went into rejoicing and worshipping mode and lost track of time. I was due to have a conference call at 10:00 am this particular morning. When I glanced at the clock, it was 10:10 am. The thought of the conference call had gone out the window. Once I finished rejoicing, I grabbed my baby and proceeded to take him for a ride on his tricycle. As I pushed him down the sidewalk, the Holy Spirit gently reminded me of my 10:00 am conference call. I turned and ran back into the house. I picked up my iPhone, and it was 10:16 am. My initial thought was, "Oh no, I'm so late!" As soon as I unlocked my iPhone, I saw a text from my coworker at 10:14 am that read, "The conference call line is down, is anyone else having issues?" Tell me God isn't good! We were all late to the 10:00 am call due to technical difficulties. See, when you are obedient and put God first, things just have a way of working out. I didn't need to make up a story as to why I was late. I was about my Father's business, and He looked out for me.

I'm sure some of my stories sound really dramatic and unbelievable, but I promise you, that is how good God is! Pray and ask God to perform the same miracles he used to perform in the Old Testament in your life today. I'm sure you've heard the cliché, "prayer changes things." Well guess what: It does! You want to see God move? Pray His Word. When you bring God's Word back to His memory, watch how fast He moves.

Reading and Applying the Word of God

The saying, "you are what you eat" remains the same as it relates to your walk with Christ. If you feed on negativity, you speak with negativity. If you feed on truth—the Word of God—then you speak the truth.

If you are ready to get on track, reading the Bible will help you to do so. *Why do I need to read the Bible?* How else will you know what God has planned for you, promised you, can do and can be in your life? All the answers to life can be found right in God's Word.

My eleven-year-old daughter told me that she had added reading the Bible to her daily schedule. I was excited for her when she told me. She asked if we could read the Bible together on the phone, but I told her she needed to make time for God on her own so that she could hear Him. Before we hung up, I informed her that it was important for her to sit and listen after she finishes reading the Bible in case God has something He wants to share with her. I advised her that it would be a good idea to write down any thoughts that come to mind after she has finished.

She called me back on FaceTime about 20 minutes later and said, "Momma, guess what! I was reading Scripture about worrying. And you know what? I was just feeling worried all morning! Now I feel like I can face my day."

My response to her was quite simple: "That was the Lord speaking to you." She smiled so big! When you invite Christ into your day through the reading of Scripture, He can be your guide.

My daughter is very shy. That particular morning, she was preparing for a Zoom session for a meeting with her classmates. My daughter told me, "Momma, sometimes we are anxious about things that don't even happen." Absolutely! That's because we are flesh and blood, human. It's in our nature to become worried.

Reading the Bible allows God's Word to offer peace, direction, comfort, wisdom, knowledge, understanding, and so much more. I often ask God to tell me His thoughts about me or inform me if I am moving in accordance with His will. He seems to always lead me to a Scripture that provides His response. This alone is reassurance that He hears me.

"Your word is a lamp to my feet and a light to my path."

Psalm 119:105

The Bible is our guide in the real world. Many people believe that we no longer have to read and understand the Old Testament. Some say we only fall under the new laws of the New Testament. If we throw out the Old Testament, we get rid of the Ten Commandments in Exodus, the songs of praise in Psalm, and the book of wisdom known as Proverbs, then we lose the reminder that God is the potter and we are the clay as explained in Jeremiah. We take away the prophecies of the coming Messiah, God's promises, and His many miracles.

In the Old Testament, you learn faith, wisdom, and a greater understanding of who God is. You learn about the fall of mankind. You realize that oftentimes, God allows the enemy to test your faith in God to demonstrate God's glory and faithfulness. The Old Testament sets the stage of life. Don't eliminate it from your reading. Many of the answers to your unanswered questions can be found there.

"Be doers of the word, and not hearers only."

James 1:22

We often go to church and hear the preacher preach his or her sermon and leave the church and go back to being our normal selves. Or we read the Bible, get convicted from what we read, but do nothing about it. Praying and reading the Bible go hand-in-hand. Instead of ignoring your convictions, talk to God, and ask Him to help you understand what it is you are doing wrong. Ask Him to help you live a righteous life that is pleasing to Him. In your weakness, God is strong.

Lamentations 3 tells us that God's grace and mercy are new each day. Each opportunity we have to take a breath of fresh air should be our motivation to try harder to lean and depend on God's strength. When you apply the Word of God to your life, you are simply reminding your spirit that you are choosing to let go of what your flesh desires to do as you walk in the purpose that God has predestined over your life.

Reading the Bible changes the way you think and the way you view things. That's why you decide to no longer hang out in the clubs, drink, party all night, and fornicate. Will you still have a desire to do these things? From time to time, the thought will cross your mind if you are not feeding on the Word. Remember, the flesh is weak. It's the Holy Spirit that is inside of you that makes the taste of sin no longer appealing. It's the same Holy Spirit that tells you not to go down that path because it only brings destruction. As you seek the Lord for help and strength, lean on John 15:7, "If you abide in Me, and My words abide in you, you will ask what you desire, and it shall be done for you."

Journal

If you haven't already, you should invest in a journal. Journaling allows you to remove thoughts from your mind and put them on paper. Use your journal to vent about bills, frustration, depression, anxieties, your spouse or children. Empty your mind of all the negativities, fears, and doubts.

"But the Helper, The Holy Spirit, who the Father will send in My name, He will teach you all things, and bring back to remembrance all things that I said to you."

John 14:26

Most sicknesses and diseases develop in our bodies as a result of stress and anxieties. Stress and anxiety come from thoughts that are in your head that you are constantly dwelling on. Many people turn to medications to assist with anxieties, stress, and depressions. If that's something you have been led to do, then I cannot give you my take on your situation.

I very often see commercials on television that feed off of a hurting America by urging the need for medications to control your non-chemically balanced emotions. Drug companies are taking advantage of our hurting society by giving us drugs that keep us down.

A friend of mine would often have panic attacks, so her primary care physician soon prescribed her Zoloft. She expressed how much worse she felt by taking the medication. It made me wonder how many other people had this same impact from such a strong narcotic. I encourage you to seek God and ask Him if you are ready to be released from your medications as you begin your healing process.

I probably have a total of eight journals. I have journals at work, in my purse, on my nightstand, near the dining room table—I just never know when I might need to release some frustration. I typically journal at the end of my day. I like to use the hour before I retire for the night as a time to revisit the events from the day with God. Understand, I speak with God throughout the day, but this is me setting time aside for just Him and I. Emptying out my thoughts into a journal before sleeping, I believe, helps me rest easier. While I'm venting, the Holy Spirit ministers to me through song and Scripture.

Remember to listen as you write. Record what you hear. God will comfort you in the midst of your pains. He always gives you good things to think about to add strength to your weariness.

After a long day, when I've finished journaling, I feel like I've ranted to my best friend. Instead of getting on the phone and gossiping, I can journal. Remember, your journal is not for the world to see. It's a conversation piece between you and the Lord. Have you ever thought, Did I hear God say that? Write down what you thought you heard. Don't mention it; just wait for confirmation. After a good night's rest, wake up and journal your dreams. Take your journal to church and write what you hear the Holy Spirit telling you through songs and the preaching or teaching of God's Word. Journaling allows you to remember and reflect. Recording what you see, think, and feel will develop your faith in knowing that you are indeed connecting with the Holy Spirit.

Fasting

"I would love to miss a meal," said no one. Isaiah 58 speaks about the importance of fasting. I remember praying and asking God if I was doing all that He required, and He led me to Scripture about fasting.

Jesus fasted. Remember when he was led into the wilderness to be tempted by the devil. While he was in the wilderness, Jesus fasted for forty days and forty nights. I'm sure you're thinking, I'm not Jesus. You are so right! Jesus was perfect. But by His strength, we can do anything. I have been trying to fast for years. It is definitely a struggle. When I should've been fasting, I would cheat and eat a snack. It took me well over five years before I was able to go 24 hours without a meal.

It's okay to take baby steps. Please don't feel like you should jump out of the ship and sink. Start by skipping your favorite meal of the day. God appreciates your initiative. If you draw closer to Him, He will draw closer to you. God honors faith and obedience.

For a while, I would fast from different things like social media, using my cellular device, watching television, or anything that I believed to be a distraction. Personally, I believe God honors these sacrifices, but Scripture defines fasting as going without food. The beauty in this is that God knows your heart. Don't get distracted by what people tell you to do. Do what you believe God is calling you to do, and be honest with yourself. The truth will set you free!

The power of fasting in Isaiah 58 indicates the ability to break bondage and obtain healing. If you are unable to move past certain situations in your life or you are in need of deliverance, try fasting.

I once fasted for 40 days. I made a chain of five links. Each link had something I wanted God to deliver me from. For my fast, I decided to skip lunch and use that time to pray over my chain for an hour each day. I began my fast in the month of January. By December of that year, God had delivered me from everything I had prayed for. I was no longer bound by those sins. Did I still have to face these temptations at some point down the road? Yes! The difference was that I had the ability to resist the temptation. I reminded myself that God had delivered me from that past sin, and I didn't have to entertain it. When someone tells you to "walk in your deliverance," that is what they mean. Tell yourself that you are no longer bound, and literally walk away from the temptation. The desire instantly goes away. I am a witness. I am grateful because I now have the victory!

Some sins are easier to resist than others. I still struggle with self-control at times, but it's not as easy for me to give in to sin as it once was. I don't walk in shame. Shame comes when you're too busy wallowing in your mistakes, taking forever to repent, and even longer to dust yourself off and try again. I don't feel condemned when I make a mistake. Instead, I quickly turn to God for forgiveness and carry on with the mission.

Remember, fasting is for growth and development. Fasting is not simply missing a meal. It's filling that hour or so with Christ. This can look like praying, reading the Bible, praising and worshiping God, or simply sitting in silence and writing what you hear the Holy Spirit saying.

Fasting Prepares You

If God is calling you to do something unexpected, go on a fast. God will prepare you for what's to come. Expect Him to show you what it is He is calling you to do. In order to be ready for your next mission, you have to be able to hear from God.

A few years ago, I moved to Kansas City. Before I left, I went on a fast for a week. During my fast, God revealed to me that he was sending me to Kansas City to prepare me for my husband. Once my fast was completed, He had revealed to me where I would live and the name of the school which my children would attend. His timing was perfect! I called the housing development in Kansas City and was told that there was one home that would become available a week before I was due to arrive. When we arrived in Kansas City, the school was due to start in two days. I spent my first day registering my children for school. If I hadn't fasted, I would have been stressed trying to figure everything out on my own.

Fasting helps you to focus on God and not be moved by distractions. Fasting makes you vulnerable and enhances your senses. You can pick up on good and bad spirits enabling you to follow God's instructions.

Jesus oftentimes separated himself from the multitude and His disciples in order to replenish Himself. When you're constantly giving of yourself, you feel drained. When you're drained, you oftentimes become cranky. How can you draw people to Christ if you're moody and cranky? If our purpose as believers is to expose the light of Christ, we can't pour from an empty cup. Utilizing the strategies in this chapter will help you focus as you take your eyes off the distractions of the world and trust God to be God. Choose today to get back on track with the purpose God has for your life. You are not here by mistake.

Reflection Time

Are you tired of dealing with the same nonsense? Make a plan for yourself and set goals. Don't give yourself a non-realistic timeline. Indicate the strategies you will use to help recognize your distractions and how you will use Scripture and Christ to overcome.

_____

_____

_____

_____

_____

_____

_____

_____

_____

_____

_____

_____

_____

_____

Epilogue

In order to be truly successful, you have to create measures for yourself to eliminate the chances for these distractions to continue. If you choose to continue to entertain your distractions, then the purpose of utilizing the tools in this book is defeated.

It will take for you to be 100% tired of dealing with the same nonsense and distraction for you to eliminate it. Don't think about how lonely you will be. Don't create a new distraction or habit that is similar to the last. Don't worry if people try to embarrass you on social media. Jesus was perfect, and He still experienced hate.

You have to want to see yourself in a better situation. You have to want more for yourself. You have to love yourself. Sometimes, we think love is buying ourselves expensive jewelry, shoes, and clothes or going on lavish getaways. Loving yourself is knowing who you are in Christ. Loving yourself is not feeling the need to put a half-naked selfie on social media. Loving yourself is demanding that you be respected and not cursed and hit.

Loving yourself is not allowing anybody to approach you any disrespectful way. Loving yourself is not being taken advantage of by creating boundaries.

Look in the mirror. Don't look, stare! Stare at yourself. Look at your scars. Look at your smile. Look at your skin tone. Look at your hair. Those things don't define you! Society wants you to believe they do. They don't! You can be as beautiful as a model, but if your heart isn't right and you are nasty with people, then all those beauty tips go out the window!

A real man is attracted to confidence; boys run from a confident woman. If a boy does approach a confident woman, he becomes insecure and doesn't know how to treat her or what to do with her. He has the problem, not you! You have nothing to prove to this insecure individual. Walk away and don't look back. Eliminate the distraction.

Jesus said in John 15 that "a servant is not greater than his master." When you are about your Father's business, the world hates you. The world hated Christ. Jesus could have used His power and authority and quit on us, but He didn't. He didn't allow the actions and behaviors of the people or even his friends to steer him off track. He continued to honor His Father.

Lose yourself in Jesus. Somehow, when you least expect it, things just work out. When you put lesser effort into trying to make every day perfect and allow God to be in control, He takes and brings you where you need to go.

Perfect practice makes perfect. You may not get it right on the first try but keep trying. Silence your phone for hours each day. Turn off the television more often. Cook at home and save money. Watch the company you keep.

You can do it! I know you can! I know, because I too was distracted. I had to get tired of going in circles, and I chose to depend on God more and more each day to show me that I can find strength in Him. I am a product of being kept by the King of kings and Lord of lords. You are loved!

"Your word have I hid in my heart that I might not sin against you."
-King David

Here's a tool I created and used to guide me during my struggle. You can use this to help you strategize against distractions.

My confession: "It's not that I am afraid; I just get easily distracted. I move hastily. I'm easily bored. Now that I am able to openly confess the truth, Lord, what must I do?"

I need a strong accountability partner.

Resist the devil, and he will flee.

Remember there is a season for everything.

Ask God:

What season am I entering?

Increase my ability to discern.

Help me to accept what the Holy Spirit displays.

Help me to be obedient.

Help me stand on Your promises.

Bring Your Word back to memory.

Show me the enemy.

Do:

Stay armed for battle.

Recognize temptation.

Read the Bible daily.

Pray constantly.

Invite the Lord to walk with me.

Think of good and positive things—truth.

Trust God.

Have faith.

Journal.

Remain encouraged.

Be quick to hear, slow to speak, slow to anger.

Seek God.

Set aside time for God daily.

Fast often.

Fellowship with like-minded people.

Move in silence.

Notes

_____

_____

_____

_____

_____

_____

_____

_____

_____

_____

_____

_____

_____

_____

_____

_____

_____

_____

_____

_____

_____

_____

_____

Let Go and Let God!

Use these pages to release your distractions to God and allow Him to fill the voided areas in your life. Remember, when you pray, expect and believe that what you request is so.

Dear God, I admit to having unbroken soul ties in my life. I loosen the soul tie between myself and (add name here and finish your prayer)

_____

_____

_____.

Dear God, help me to let go of (list distraction)

_____

_____

_____.

Dear God, teach me to wait for instructions and walk in obedience concerning

_____

_____

_____.

Dear God, I have many fears, but I know you are my protector. Lord, please take away my fears and replace them with peace.

_____

_____

_____.

Dear God, I admit to having unbroken soul ties in my life. I loosen the soul tie between myself and (add name here and finish your prayer)

_____

_____

_____.

Dear God, help me to let go of (list distraction)

_____

_____

_____.

Dear God, teach me to wait for instructions and walk in obedience concerning

_____

_____

_____.

Dear God, I have many fears, but I know you are my protector. Lord, please take away my fears and replace them with peace.

_____

_____

_____.

Precious Father, I am grateful for your many blessings. Here are few things you have done for me today:

_____

_____

_____

About the Author

Author, songwriter, playwright, actress—the list goes on! Rachiel Renea is a woman of God who loves to spread the Good News. She is the Founder and President of Blossomed for Purpose, a nonprofit organization which provides support for single mothers and their daughters through mentorship programs, finance workshops, adult education, and spiritual development.

Through trial and error, mostly error, Rachiel Renea decided to apply the teachings from the Scriptures to her everyday life to see if there would be a significant change in the outcome in her relationships, finances, and personal development. With each exciting blessing, whether peaceful gain or personal growth, she felt inspired to share her amazing experiences with women everywhere. Her transparency allows her readers and anyone she encounters to easily connect and relate to her as she shares the hurtful trials that she endured that either pushed her closer to God or drew her farther from His presence.

Rachiel Renea is a native of Charlotte, North Carolina. She is a loving, devoted mother of two sons and one daughter. She is a graduate of the University of Phoenix where she obtained her Associates Degree in Criminal Justice. She attended North Carolina Central University in Durham, North Carolina where she studied Political Science. She is a Staff Sergeant in the Active Army Reserve, where she works as a Human Resources Sergeant with over thirteen years of service.

Connect with Rachiel Renea

Website: www.rachielrenea.co
Facebook: @rachielrenea
Instagram: @Rachiel_Renea

Blossomed for Purpose (nonprofit)
Website: www.womenoffire.org
Facebook: @blossomedforpurpose
Instagram: @blossomedforpurpose

Podcast: "Blossomed for Purpose" with Rachiel Renea